SOWERS OF LIFE

How Farmers Shape Our World

GURVINDER SINGH GHUMAN

BLUEROSE PUBLISHERS
India | U.K.

Copyright © Gurvinder Singh Ghuman 2024

All rights reserved by author. No part of this publication may be reproduced, stored in a retrieval system or transmitted in any form or by any means, electronic, mechanical, photocopying, recording or otherwise, without the prior permission of the author. Although every precaution has been taken to verify the accuracy of the information contained herein, the publisher assume no responsibility for any errors or omissions. No liability is assumed for damages that may result from the use of information contained within.

BlueRose Publishers takes no responsibility for any damages, losses, or liabilities that may arise from the use or misuse of the information, products, or services provided in this publication.

For permissions requests or inquiries regarding this publication, please contact:

BLUEROSE PUBLISHERS
www.BlueRoseONE.com
info@bluerosepublishers.com
+91 8882 898 898
+4407342408967

ISBN: 978-93-6261-805-4

Cover design: Tahira
Typesetting: Tanya Raj Upadhyay

First Edition: October 2024

'Dedicated to all those farmers who, generation after generation, despite challenges like droughts and floods, have protected the pride of the nation by strengthening the food security of the country with crops like gold grown by sweat.'

Disclaimer:

All statistics and figures used in this book have been collected from various sources. The author and publisher accept no responsibility for any errors, inaccuracies, or issues of any kind. If the content of this book offends anyone's feelings, the author expresses regret, as the intention is not to hurt anyone's sentiments.

Table of Contents

If There Are Farmers, There Is a World.............................. 1

Farmers' Movement and Solutions...................................... 5

Livelihood and life crisis caused by a flawed market 9

Listen to the Farmer, Then Reflect................................... 11

First Listen to the Farmer, Then Understand the Problem 44

If There Are Farmers, There Is a World

Author: Gurvinder Singh Ghuman
My Views
Farmers are burdened by an imperfect market system.

Historically, this country has endured centuries of exploitation. Invaders and local rulers alike came to exploit its agricultural wealth. From princely state ministers to landlords, everyone took advantage of the farmers, focusing on rent collection and neglecting farmers' welfare. Farmers have suffered the most from floods, droughts, and famines. Post-independence, numerous agricultural reform schemes and laws were introduced, but they often fell short. Land consolidation efforts haven't prevented ongoing land fragmentation due to family divisions, forcing many rural families to migrate to cities for better opportunities. Large landowners are often concerned about the government imposing restrictions on their land size and the possibility of confiscation. Therefore, it is crucial to reassure them that the boundaries of their land will remain intact and unaltered.

The motivation behind writing this book is to advocate for a perfect market for farmers, ensuring they receive fair compensation for their hard work without excessive taxes. Middlemen often take a significant portion of farmers' profits, and unpredictable weather further exacerbates their financial instability. Farmers struggle with heavy rains, floods, locust infestations, and fluctuating market prices.

These challenges sometimes force farmers to abandon their produce on the roads or destroy it because they can't afford to transport it to the market. Consequently, many farmers face insurmountable debts, leading to tragic outcomes like suicides. Cash crops come with high production costs, driven up by rising prices of fertilizers, seeds, and diesel.

I believe that if the government can create a more efficient market, farmers will be adequately compensated, and farming costs will decrease. Improving rural infrastructure, especially roads and affordable transportation, will significantly benefit farmers. Ensuring prompt payment for crops will solve many of their problems. In our country, farming is not treated as a business, and farmers are often unversed in market dynamics. When there is a surplus crop, neither the farmer nor the consumer benefits, leading to questions about who actually profits. The government must address this issue seriously.

My Views on "Farmer to the World" by Gurvinder Singh Ghuman

I believe the market should be fully optimized. Eliminating middlemen could resolve many of the farmers' issues. Currently, there is a need for extensive grain storage facilities so that farmers don't have to sell their crops immediately at low prices. This book seeks to answer such questions. If these issues are discussed nationally, farmers' problems can be addressed. Moving forward from the repeal of the three reform laws due to the farmers' movement, we should include inputs from farmer organizations, intellectuals, and agricultural experts. As our population exceeds one and a half billion in the 21st century, agricultural reforms are essential to feed everyone and increase farmers' incomes.

Making the Indian Market Fully Effective

The central government has implemented three agricultural reform laws aimed at improving the agricultural sector. Prime Minister Narendra Modi and Agriculture Minister Narendra Singh Tomar claim these laws will transform farmers' lives. However, some farmer organizations argue that these laws harm agriculture and demand their repeal. This article aims to explore the government's intent behind these laws and the reasons for farmers' opposition.

The current Indian market suffers from disorder, immaturity, and unethical competition. A lack of transparency and honesty means buyers and sellers are not accountable to each other. Buyers exploit these flaws, affecting farmers' incomes and crop prices. Similar issues affect the wages of laborers and fees for professionals, leading to wasted earnings in an unregulated market. This chaotic structure converts potential profits into average or minimal returns over time, making it difficult for all classes to survive. Their livelihoods are endangered, affecting families and communities, resulting in a dysfunctional market.

The reform laws were created with good intentions to uplift farmers, but fears of a directionless market led to their rejection. The immature market conditions mean the benefits of these reforms are not immediately apparent. I suggest maintaining the current system, including MSP purchases of wheat, paddy, and other crops, for the next four years. This period would allow farmers to feel secure while the government, policymakers, and farmer organizations fully analyze the reforms.

Unhealthy market competition prevents fair distribution of services, remuneration, and income. To mitigate income losses, the government resorts to discounts, subsidies, economic incentives, loans, and loan waivers. The government aims to promote self-reliance and implement agricultural reforms for farmers' upliftment. However, discussions with farmers reveal the imperfect market's impact and the suffering it causes. Farmers' demands to repeal these laws are a struggle for their survival. The flawed market underlies many national issues, causing conflicts between the central government and farmers. The problem lies not with farmers but with buyers who also suffer under these immature market conditions.

Today, Indian consumers have money, but the business system struggles to earn it. Farmers, traders, laborers, professionals, business institutions, and others affected by this system seek freedom from it. The question arises: What defines an ideal complete market versus a flawed market? What negative impacts does this flawed market have on the country and its sectors? Conversely, what positive impacts would a complete market bring? A nationwide discussion involving government, political sectors, agricultural experts, universities, and seminars could provide answers. Though complex, collective effort towards establishing a complete market is possible. Better coordination and market discipline are needed, but together we can create a beneficial market for everyone.

Farmers' Movement and Solutions

In an effort to enact comprehensive reforms, the Central Government has introduced three significant laws aimed at transforming the agricultural sector. The urgent need is to enhance productivity and ensure farmers receive a fair price for their hard work. However, it is crucial to understand the farmers' current situation and address their concerns about insecurity. Addressing these key points could help resolve the ongoing discontent among farmers. Agricultural reforms are necessary in this evolving and competitive era. Here are some important considerations:

1. There is no consistent scale of production for grains, fruits, oilseeds, pulses, and vegetables across the country, as productivity varies by geography, environment, and weather. Crop prices are also unstable. While farmers may profit in some years, they may only break even or incur losses in others. Addressing these concerns is essential before implementing reforms.

2. The main issue isn't opposition to agricultural reform laws but rather market insecurity. There is unhealthy competition, and the market lacks planning and transparency, preventing farmers from getting fair prices. Farmers fear the involvement of private players in agriculture, adding to their insecurity.

3. Not all farmers benefit from support prices nationwide. In regions like Punjab, Haryana, and Western Uttar Pradesh, government purchases of wheat and paddy provide income security. Consequently, farmers in these areas prioritize these crops over cash crops, contributing to their opposition to reforms.

4. The market for fruits and vegetables is driven by consumer needs and preferences, yet it remains poorly planned. Farmers lack knowledge of commercial production and storage, and there is insufficient warehousing, transport, and cold storage facilities. This limits market expansion and forces farmers to sell their produce locally at low prices.

5. Agricultural-based industries are underdeveloped in producing states, leading to incomplete agro-industrial growth. Had there been a focus on developing these industries three decades ago, farmers would have received fair prices, leading to prosperity and increased exports. The current conflict between farmers and the government could have been avoided.

6. The ongoing conflict between farmers and the government has lasted two years, creating unnecessary disputes. This initiative should have received positive responses. The goal is to reach a consensus, and I offer some responsible suggestions to avoid further conflict:

a. Delay implementing or repealing the three reform laws for three years. Then, implement agreed-upon reforms experimentally over the next three years after thorough discussion.

b. Ensure farmers do not feel at risk by maintaining the minimum support price (MSP) and continuing government purchases of wheat and paddy where currently applicable for the next three years.

c. Farmers should receive prices for their crops that are not lower than international prices.

7. While there are beneficial aspects of the reform laws, it's crucial to implement them with farmers' consent. Utilize global agricultural research and modern technology to benefit Indian farmers. Establish ideal markets and networks for selling grains, vegetables, fruits, and oilseeds across the country.

8. To make farming profitable and increase farmers' incomes in the 21st century, private players should be involved under government supervision. This will help meet the country's food grain needs despite limited land holdings and prepare farmers to compete with international prices.

9. The width of roads connecting villages is inadequate in many states. Setting a minimum width standard will benefit village infrastructure development and prevent future issues with road expansions.

10. Governments currently provide financial support to landowners through various means, but if these facilities become unavailable in the future, what will happen to the farmers? Discussions are needed on when farmers will become self-sufficient.

11. Farmers need to be aware of climate change risks and prepared for crops that can withstand extreme weather and conserve groundwater.

All segments of society, including the government, farmers' organizations, and citizens, are concerned about farmers' welfare. Instead of conflict, everyone should work towards creating a positive environment and better direction.

Conclusion

The flawed market system is the root of many problems, leading to conflicts between the central government and farmers. This system and the buyers exploit crop prices, affecting farmers' earnings and wages for laborers and professionals. The entire country, not just protesting farmers, seeks change. It's time to create a healthy, competitive, disciplined, mature, ethical, complete, and ideal market, which will automatically address most of the country's issues.

Livelihood and life crisis caused by a flawed market

The economy that has developed in the country under the guise of globalization and liberalization has dismantled the traditional economic structure that once provided employment and livelihood to millions. In this new system, the wealthy have become wealthier while the poor have become poorer. There has been a steady decline in profits, wages, and benefits in the labor-driven sectors. This has led to a chaotic market environment, where skilled workers, traders, hawkers, shopkeepers in the retail sector, and farmers all struggle to receive fair compensation for their labor and products despite their hard work. Small production units and the agricultural sector, both striving for survival, have to spend on fuel, interest, electricity, and rent to stay afloat, but profits have not kept pace with rising costs. Consequently, the working population not only faces a livelihood crisis but also suffers as consumers in this troubled economy.

In reality, the current Indian market is plagued by undisciplined, immature, unethical, and unhealthy competition. The lack of transparency within the system results in a lack of accountability between buyers and sellers. Consequently, large buyers exploit these inconsistencies, manipulating farmers' incomes and crop prices. Similarly, sellers' profits, laborers' wages, and professionals' and skilled workers' earnings are adversely affected. This leads to the hard-earned money of these groups being lost to the uncontrolled and incomplete market. Over time, the country's fair and profitable economic structure devolves into one of average or minimal profit due to inherent contradictions, raising market costs. Such conditions make survival difficult for all classes, endangering their livelihoods. As a result, the lives of their families and communities are pushed to the brink of crisis. Ultimately, this chaotic structure has turned the market into a diseased entity, festering over time.

In the true sense, the country's farmers are suffering the most from this unjust system. The consistently declining profits from their produce illustrate this issue. As a result, many farmers, facing continuous financial losses, are tragically driven to suicide. Instead of addressing the root cause, the government provides economic support through subsidies, incentives, loans, and minimum support prices. However, these measures fail to effectively resolve the problem due to the uncontrolled market. With low income, farmers rely on loans and subsidies to cover household expenses, leading to an inability to repay these loans. Consequently, they become trapped in debt, often having to mortgage their farms and homes after being declared defaulters by banks. Essentially, the loans and mortgaged assets of farmers are sustaining the banks.

Listen to the Farmer, Then Reflect

The farmer movement that lasted about a year may have succeeded in repealing the three agricultural reform laws proposed by the Central Government, but it has also likely hindered the implementation of any new reformist laws for the next decade. Political parties seeking farmer votes might celebrate the Central Government's defeat, but in truth, the farmers have lost an opportunity for essential reforms. Agricultural reforms are crucial for addressing the needs of the 21st century, feeding the country's 1.4 billion people, and increasing farmers' incomes.

Undoubtedly, the movement, largely led by farmers from Punjab, Haryana, and Uttar Pradesh near Delhi, was one of the longest farmer protests in India. The government's approach towards the movement was not constructive. Even if the government's intentions were right, it failed to effectively communicate the benefits of the reforms to the farmers. At a time when the country's economy is unstable, is it wise to tamper with the minimum support price (MSP)? When farmers believe the reforms are against their interests, they should have been informed about the true nature of these changes. Why do farmers feel that the government does not adopt a liberal approach in a democratic system? Why does the government not demonstrate sensitivity and magnanimity? Farmers are questioning why these bills were introduced secretly during the Corona crisis and passed hastily. Why was there a need to amend the 'Essential Commodities Act'?

The commercialization of agriculture has adversely affected small farmers worldwide. Can this model work in a country like India with small landholdings? Global statistics show that commercialization often leads to farmers losing their land. In India, agriculture is not just an industry; it is a part of the farmer's identity. Land is passed down through generations, making its value inestimable. Farming is already unprofitable for many, and numerous farmers rent their land. They feared that the new system would push them out of agriculture.

The government should work to alleviate these fears and listen to the farmers' real concerns. Ideally, these reforms should have been preceded by a nationwide debate, taking into account the opinions of the farmers affected by the changes. Since agriculture is a state subject, there should have been extensive discussions with state governments. India is a democracy, and oligarchic practices cannot be developed. Some farmer organizations believe that the reforms should have been postponed and reintroduced in a new format after thorough discussions. While it is true that 21st-century agriculture cannot operate with 16th-century methods, farmers' trust and opinions must be prioritized. Long-term movements are detrimental to society and the country.

Haryana and Punjab have been at the forefront of agricultural reforms. Punjab, in particular, benefitted from major post-independence development projects like the Bhakra and

Nangal dams. These states were the first to benefit from the Green Revolution due to water availability, and they also gained from the MSP. This is why the movement had a more significant impact in these areas. In regions without MSP benefits, similar protests were not observed. Political reasons and caste identity, which have historically shown opposition to the government, are also underlying factors in this movement. Consequently, some farmers in Haryana and Punjab feel that the current government does not represent their interests.

The Farmer Cultivates Sorrows

Every leader calls India an agriculture-based country, but when it comes to budget presentations, finance ministers prioritize industry over agriculture. They proclaim the nation's agricultural foundation, yet fail to make agriculture beneficial for the country. In reality, 52 percent of the population, or about 60 crore people, depend directly and indirectly on agriculture. The last census indicates a decline in the agriculture-dependent population, with a significant rise in landless farmers—around 35 crore are landless, while about 25 crore are actual farmers.

Agriculture contributes 14 percent to the GDP. There is a narrative that agriculture's share in GDP is declining. Without fair pricing for farmers, this decline is inevitable. Lower incomes naturally result in a reduced GDP share, a situation that has been deliberately engineered.

The World Bank, influential in global economic policies, advocates for farmers to leave agriculture and work in industries. A World Bank report criticized the government for not removing farmers from agriculture and suggested accelerating land acquisition. It proposed that land should be taken from those deemed unfit and that young people with agricultural backgrounds should be trained for industrial jobs. This is part of a strategic effort to move people away from agriculture.

Discussions rarely focus on farmers' costs and profits. When the system aims to drive people away from agriculture, what can be expected? We have adopted a flawed American model, failing to invest in the public sector and keeping agricultural product prices low to push farmers out of farming and into labor roles. Farmers have never received fair prices or efforts to reduce their costs. For instance, wheat prices rose from Rs. 76 per quintal in 1970 to Rs. 1450 per quintal in 2015, a 19-fold increase over 45 years. In contrast, government employees' salaries increased by 120 to 150 times, college teachers' salaries by 120 to 150 times, and primary teachers' salaries by 280 to 300 times. Employees receive 108 types of allowances, while farmers receive none. They cultivate not crops, but sorrows.

Farmers' anger often manifests in movements, which the government and politicians quell with promises. If this continues, a major uprising is inevitable. The truth is that agriculture is being neglected, and farmers are being forced out of farming.

The core issue in Indian agriculture is economic mismanagement, rooted in economic insecurity. Year after year, farmers suffer from unfair pricing, while the government controls grain prices for political gain, keeping the middle class happy with cheap grains. But what is being given to the farmers who produce these grains? They are being driven out of farming, deprived of fair prices.

The problem of farmer suicides has two facets: the true extent of these suicides is not fully known, and most suicides occur where crop uncertainty is highest, especially with cash crops like grapes and cotton. In regions like Vidarbha and Bundelkhand, and even Punjab, the full extent of the crisis is emerging due to increased awareness. Cases of severe farmer suicides are reported in many states, including Orissa.

The cost of cash crops is rising, but policymakers are not addressing the looming challenge of feeding a population approaching 1.5 billion. Grain imports began in the 1970s, a period known as 'ship to mouth,' where grains were unloaded from ships directly for consumption. The Green Revolution ended these imports, but current policies risk repeating history. Feeding such a large population through imports is unsustainable and compromises national security, which is closely tied to food security. The global food crisis of 2007-08 led to food riots in 37 countries, but India was unaffected due to its robust system. We must not overlook the importance of maintaining this strength.

It is often said that after the Green Revolution, farmers' problems have worsened due to the neglect of traditional crops and the emphasis on water-intensive crops. However, the real issue lies in the costs involved. Before the Green Revolution, traditional Indian crops were insufficient to feed the entire country. The Green Revolution introduced two key measures: the establishment of minimum support prices

(MSP) for crops, which increased farmers' confidence in the system, and the creation of the Food Corporation of India (FCI). Managing the procurement, handling, and distribution of food grains across such a large country was a significant challenge. Despite corruption being a major issue, dismantling this system would be disastrous, potentially returning us to a 'ship to mouth' situation. It is crucial to consider production costs and ensure that farmers receive fair prices. If farmers were paid prices adjusted for inflation, many who moved to cities might return to farming. Providing market prices for grains and covering additional costs through their 'Jan Dhan accounts' is essential.

Some argue that raising the price of farmers' grains will lead to inflation. In India, 60 crore people are involved in agriculture, and in half of the states, farmers' monthly income is less than Rs. 1700. This amount is insufficient even to support a cow. In discussions about a minimum living wage, farmers must also be included. Farmers are both producers and consumers. If we provide farmers with incomes that match their expenditures, it would boost our GDP. This would make the slogan 'Sabka Saath, Sabka Vikas' truly meaningful. Ensuring minimum support prices can provide real security for farmers. The Shanta Kumar Committee report indicates that only 6 percent of farmers benefit from MSP, leaving 94 percent without any safety net. This lack of security explains why many farmers resort to desperate measures, including suicide.

The Plight Due to Decline in Income

The imperfection of the rural economy's market has turned farming into an unprofitable venture. Agriculture can no longer be seen as a profitable sector. This decline in income affects not only farming but also related non-agricultural sectors. The situation reached its lowest point during the recent Corona crisis, resulting in the loss of millions of jobs. Despite these hardships, discontent does not appear to flare up in Indian rural society, likely due to the tradition of joint families and a culture of contentment. It is estimated that employment opportunities in rural areas have decreased compared to cities in recent years. The survival of rural India despite such a severe crisis can be considered a miraculous event, as social peace would typically be at risk given the high unemployment rates.

For the past two decades, India's agricultural sector has faced multiple crises, although the situation was not significantly better before. A study by the United Nations Conference on Trade and Development reveals that, after adjusting for inflation, the prices farmers receive for their produce have remained almost unchanged globally between 1985 and 2005. The reality is that agricultural income has been stagnant for the last four decades. This stagnation has frustrated farmers, leading the younger generation to seek ways out of farming. Farmers and their descendants have come to believe that their fate is to be born in debt, live in debt, and die in debt.

The Challenge of Establishing a Fair Price

Uncontrolled market forces have led to a situation where farmers neither receive a fair price nor the full value for their produce. This issue is not unique to India; it is a global trend. For example, in the 1980s in America, farmers used to earn a profit of thirty-seven cents for every dollar of produce sold, but today they earn only fifteen cents. This reduction in profit is primarily due to the dominance of large corporations, which take away profits from common farmers and small shopkeepers.

Various studies highlight the need to make market policies economically viable and address the factors causing market chaos. These factors point to the urgent need for effective market regulations, as they are driving many small shopkeepers to the brink of extinction. Examining markets across India reveals that farmers suffer due to open market policies, while efforts are made to eliminate small shopkeepers. The notion that farmers can sell their produce anywhere in the open market undermines the rights of local shopkeepers, leading to landlessness among small farmers and driving shopkeepers to seek other businesses due to dwindling profits.

In recent decades, the Central Government's adoption of global liberalization policies has led to increased control by large capitalists. Major retail market players exploit these policies, manipulating market prices by stockpiling goods, which decreases the profits of small traders. Consequently, farmers also fail to benefit from their production costs. The aggressive promotion of the open market benefits only a few large businessmen. Due to this imperfect market, farmers cannot secure a fair price for their produce. This market does not support agricultural growth. Despite the government's policies and subsidies, farmers' incomes continue to decline, pushing them to protest and leading to disappointment and frustration, often resulting in suicides within the agricultural sector. If the market were properly regulated, farmers could receive fair prices for their crops.

Understand the Concern of Farmers!

In early April, farmers from across the country gathered in large numbers in Delhi, staging a significant movement reminiscent of the historic 13-month-long farmers' protest at the Delhi borders. This recent assembly underscores the numerous difficulties farmers face, highlighting a deepening economic crisis in agriculture. Those in power need to recognize this crisis with sensitivity. It is hoped that the leaders in Delhi sensed the collective anguish from Kashmir to Kanyakumari, as reflected by the large crowd at Ramlila Maidan. It is also worth questioning why mainstream media gave this movement scant attention and why those who contribute significantly to the country's economy are marginalized in today's flood of information. The increasing economic inequality in the country further confirms this marginalization.

Addressing visible and invisible agricultural problems like unemployment and inflation is essential. Besides farmers, many economists and agricultural experts have voiced concerns over significant cuts in programs like MNREGA in the Union Budget. The unresolved issue of minimum support price guarantees traps farmers in debt. The rising costs of crop production, without a corresponding increase in income, have turned farming into a loss-making venture. In March, farmers and tribals in Maharashtra protested against the sharp drop in prices for onions, potatoes, and other agricultural products.

Additionally, farmers today are heavily impacted by natural calamities. Climate change-induced seasonal variations have made crop damage a persistent issue. The destruction of Rabi crops in April 2023, just before harvest, was particularly devastating because the farmers had already incurred all production costs. Landless and small farmers, who farm on leased land, were hit hardest. These farmers, having paid for the land contracts with expensive loans, do not even receive compensation for crop losses.

The government must sincerely adopt a welfare approach. Identifying landless farmers and formulating policies to protect their interests is crucial. The impact of climate change on these farmers should be addressed sensitively. The government should act as a guardian, devising separate plans for the welfare of poor farmers. As the country's population exceeds 140 crore, failing to address the issues faced by farmers threatens food security. Climate change has already jeopardized our food security. The Russia-Ukraine war has triggered a global food crisis, from which India must learn. Eliminating grain black marketing and improving air-conditioned storage facilities are necessary. Adequate grain storage will prevent farmers from being forced to sell their produce immediately after harvest, ensuring they get fair prices. Addressing the shortage of food grain storage in the country should be a priority to help farmers secure better returns for their produce.

Disillusionment with farming due to losses

Farmers in the country face numerous challenges, including crises related to weather and global warming. They also struggle with an imperfect market, which often prevents them from receiving fair compensation for their labor. When farmers do not receive a fair price for their efforts and rightful earnings, they incur significant losses. To cover these losses, they repeatedly take out loans. If they manage to secure a bank loan, it is manageable, but if not, they fall prey to moneylenders and loan sharks. The inability to repay these loans leads to severe consequences, including social humiliation and, tragically, suicides. The increasing costs of farming exacerbate this situation. According to the National Crime Records Bureau, between 1995 and the subsequent twenty years, 318,528 farmers committed suicide, with debt burdens being a primary cause. This trend has continued in recent years, eroding the farming culture.

Children from farming families are increasingly abandoning agriculture. Young women are reluctant to marry farmers' sons, recognizing farming as a losing proposition. Farmers are trapped in a cycle of debt, and their children are migrating to cities, seeking livelihoods through small jobs. In many agriculture-centric states like Haryana, Punjab, and Uttar Pradesh, the low profitability of farming is a key reason for the difficulty in finding brides for farmers' sons. The arduous labor and low income from agriculture and horticulture deter girls from rural marriages.

Unfortunately, agricultural policies in India focus more on increasing crop production rather than boosting farmers' incomes. While the government aims to maintain robust food grain stocks, it neglects to enhance farmers' earnings, leaving them vulnerable to market forces. International organizations like the World Bank, influenced by wealthy nations, also push market-centric policies on developing countries. In 2015, the World Bank suggested that the Indian government relocate 400 million people from villages to cities over the next 20 years. These "agricultural refugees" now populate urban slums, undertaking any available work to survive.

Income should be enough to live!

The annual income of the average farmer in the country is so low that it makes living a simple life nearly impossible. A survey conducted a few years ago across seventeen states found that the average farmer's income was less than twenty thousand rupees, reflecting the situation for nearly half the country. Alarmingly, this amount is equivalent to just one of the 108 types of allowances provided under the Seventh Pay Commission. Additionally, data from the National Sample Survey Office in 2016 highlighted a significant disparity between the income of farmers and other social classes. Despite this, the issue has not sparked serious discussion in the country. This raises doubts about whether the Central Government's promise to double farmers' incomes by 2022 is feasible, especially given the current Ukraine-Russia conflict, global recession, and the ongoing COVID-19 crisis.

The significant income gap among different social classes largely stems from a market-driven economic system. Agriculture data from the Central Statistics Office confirms this, showing that the Gross Value Added Index hit its lowest level in 14 years during the October-December period of 2018. This indicates a decline in agricultural incomes, a reality that has not elicited much concern among farmers. The agricultural sector has been in a dire state for years, and the failure of measures to address its decline has been largely overlooked, treated as a normal occurrence.

Growing losses

A study by the Organization for Co-operation and Development, in collaboration with the Indian Council for Research on International Economic Relations, assessed the total losses suffered by farmers between 2000-01 and 2016-17. It found that the agriculture sector endured a staggering loss of Rs 45 lakh crore due to farmers not receiving fair prices for their produce. Additionally, a study by NITI Aayog estimated that the real income of farmers increased by only 0.44 percent from 2011-12 to 2015-16. It is believed that farmer income growth has been nearly zero in the two years following 2016. This situation prompted the government to introduce the 'Direct Income Support' initiative, known as the 'Pradhan Mantri Kisan Yojana.' Under this scheme, Rs. 6000 is deposited directly into the bank accounts of small farmers annually.

Pricing should stand the test of justice

It is ironic that the country's food providers also suffer the consequences of weather damage. Even with a good harvest, farmers often do not receive a fair price for their crops. This is due to the imbalance in the market's supply and demand principles. Frequently, farmers end up destroying their crops in the fields because they can't get a fair price. It has become common for farmers to throw tomatoes, potatoes, and onions on the roads when they can't sell them profitably. Newspapers often report that farmers are not getting a fair market price, leading to a drop in retail prices for those commodities.

The 'Dalwai Commission,' tasked with finding ways to double farmers' incomes, has proposed a new formula through the 'Commission for Agricultural Costs and Prices.' This involves calculating the production costs of Rabi and Kharif crops and comparing them with the income per crop. However, an agriculture magazine has revealed some alarming facts, showing that farmers do not even receive half the production cost per hectare for wheat and paddy in the markets.

It is widely known that only a small fraction of farmers in the country benefit from the minimum support price (MSP) for certain crops. The Shanta Kumar Committee's report highlights that only 6 percent of the country's farmers receive MSP. Farmer leaders argue that announcing MSP neither helps set the consumer price for flour nor guarantees that farmers will receive the declared price. The primary goal of the CACP formula, which determines MSP, is to ensure farmers get the set price without causing inflationary pressure on the economy. However, government economic policies are a significant factor in the current agricultural crisis. To keep food prices low, MSP is often set below production costs, making agriculture unprofitable. When comparing farmers' incomes to inflation, any increase appears negligible. The government should rationalize MSP determination and ensure farmers receive a fair price for their crops.

The Reality of Minimum Support Price

The reality of the minimum support price (MSP) for crops in India is that it mainly benefits only two or three crops and a mere 6 percent of farmers. Ensuring MSP for a wider range of crops and genuinely doubling farmers' incomes is crucial. Achieving this requires transparency and a sensitive approach from the country's leadership. The government needs to act quickly on its promise to guarantee MSP, as the delay has led farmers to consider renewed agitation.

Farmers have called for a nationwide movement against the central government for not legally guaranteeing MSP. Farmer leaders claim that the promise of a legal guarantee for MSP was a key reason they agreed to end their 18-month-long protest. They point out that the government had assured the formation of a committee to provide this legal guarantee.

Although the government announces MSP for 23 crops each year, only around 6 percent of farmers actually sell their paddy and wheat to government agencies. This means about 94 percent of the country's farmers do not benefit from MSP. Such treatment of the country's food providers is unjust, as farmers are the backbone of India's food security mission. It is hoped that the central government will soon fulfill its promise of a legal MSP guarantee and introduce the necessary legislation in the next Parliament session. Farmers argue that purchasing agricultural produce below the MSP should be legally punishable. They also demand that MSP be calculated using the 'C2 formula' and that the recommendations of the Dr. M.S. Swaminathan committee be honestly implemented. Governments need to be held accountable for ensuring MSP.

Currently, the government maintains MSP to control inflation and support small farmers, primarily setting MSP for Kharif and Rabi crops. The question arises whether MSP should also cover other crops besides wheat and rice. Without democratic pressure, governments might abandon the MSP facility, a concern that gained traction during past farmers' movements. This is why farmers continually demand a legal MSP guarantee. Smallholding farmers cannot be left to market forces alone. Even though only 6 percent of farmers currently benefit from MSP, eliminating it could create severe market conditions. Various governments have sought alternatives to MSP, but abolishing it could threaten the existence of small farmers. This raises questions about why major initiatives to boost farmers' incomes have not materialized and whether the promise to double farmers' incomes by 2022 has been fulfilled. Real income should be assessed considering inflation. According to the National Sample Survey Office, the estimated monthly income of farmer families in 2018-19 was just Rs 10,218, while costs for agricultural inputs like fertilizers, pesticides, and diesel have nearly doubled in recent years.

The government must enhance the current MSP scheme and ensure it is more effective, extending its benefits to as many farmers as possible across all 23 crops covered by MSP. The lack of government accountability regarding MSP forces farmers to demand a legal guarantee.

We understand the significant agricultural challenges facing the country. Increasing farmers' incomes is essential for alleviating poverty and improving their quality of life. This requires addressing the agricultural crisis with a humane approach. For many in India, farming is not just an economic activity but a way of life passed down through generations. As Gandhi said, "the soul of India lives in its villages," reflecting the deep cultural and historical importance of farming.

Farmers should be represented in policy-making committees and organizations to ensure that policies are made with their consent and in their best interests. When neither farmers nor consumers receive fair prices, it is crucial to investigate who benefits from this disparity. Research is needed to understand the underlying issues causing the agricultural crisis. If timely action is not taken, the country's food chain could be at risk.

Uncontrolled Market - Failed Subsidy Approach

The subsidy system in Indian agriculture was introduced to protect farmers from market fluctuations, but its effectiveness remains questionable due to the uncontrolled market. Despite governmental efforts to halt the continuous decline in farmers' agricultural income, these measures have not proven beneficial in reality. Most of the subsidies intended for farmers end up benefiting large companies instead.

To genuinely help farmers through subsidies, the agricultural market needs restructuring. Making the agricultural market profitable in a practical sense could revive its vitality. However, leaving farmers at the mercy of the open market will not reduce their dissatisfaction or sense of insecurity. Agriculture must become practically profitable to restore prosperity to the fields and barns. This exploitation is a global issue. For example, Africa, which produces 75 percent of the cocoa beans for chocolate, remains impoverished while America and Europe flourish. African farmers receive only two percent of the revenue, condemning them to poverty.

The instability in agricultural product prices has driven Indian farmers to protest in recent years. Larger retailers have a significant role in price determination, but competition and major retail markets often exploit farmers, preventing them from benefiting. Ensuring fair and guaranteed prices for farmers is the biggest challenge today and needs to be addressed urgently.

Market interference has exacerbated the crisis for farmers. Without guaranteed profitable prices, the freedom to sell crops anywhere cannot uplift farmers' morale. Instead of pushing agribusiness towards market reforms that cater to industry needs, India should develop a system that genuinely supports farmers' economic self-reliance. A food system based on local production, procurement, and distribution is essential. Strengthening the existing network of agricultural produce market committees and creating a robust trade system that offers maximum selling prices to attract farmers is crucial for achieving this goal.

Farmers in Market Trouble

Many farmer organizations, both in India and globally, believe that market policies and practical challenges are pushing small farmers out of agriculture. The continuous subdivision of land among family members and the increasing cost of seeds, fertilizers, and petroleum products have rendered agricultural production unprofitable. The open market poses significant risks, with small farmers losing their land under the guise of being able to sell produce anywhere. This was a key issue in the recent year-long farmers' protest in India. Farmers in Western countries share similar concerns about the open market and the freedom of large retailers to stockpile produce, a concern echoed by Indian farmers.

As a result, many farmers' children are abandoning agriculture for urban areas, recognizing that agriculture in India is more of a livelihood than a business. The fact that over 50% of the population relies on agriculture underscores this reality. The government, under pressure from big capitalists, is hastily liberalizing the agricultural market without understanding farmers' practical difficulties. This overzealous approach by the central government is causing farmers to doubt their intentions. If market liberalization truly benefited farmers, those in Europe and America wouldn't be struggling today while capitalists thrive. The agricultural crisis in Western countries illustrates the failure of these policies.

Questions about these policies arose after the Uruguay Round of talks and the establishment of the World Trade

Organization in the late 20th century. Western countries have exacerbated the situation by providing substantial subsidies to their farmers, making it impossible for Indian farmers to compete with subsidized American agricultural products. India and other developing countries have consistently highlighted this unfair subsidy issue at international forums. If these market policies were effective, American and European farmers wouldn't face crises.

The reality is that farmers' incomes have declined relative to their costs and market inflation. This is evident when comparing farmers' incomes to those in other sectors. To offset these losses, Western countries provide subsidies to keep their agricultural products competitive globally. Alarmingly, 80% of these government subsidies go to trading companies. Without these subsidies, their exports would drop by 40%.

The Farmer Embracing Death

While the stock market reaches record highs and the economy is touted as one of the fastest-growing in the world, the harsh reality is that the number and rate of suicides in the country are rising. Tragically, farmers, along with workers, are increasingly among those taking their own lives. Crop destruction from seasonal calamities and low prices due to high production contribute to the farmer's hardships, highlighting their plight and insecurity. This situation exposes both the indifference of the government and the insensitivity of society, which fails to protect and support these hardworking individuals.

A recent Niti Aayog report indicates that 85% of the country's workforce is employed in the informal sector. Their labor fuels industrial growth, boosts the economy, and drives up the stock market. Yet, the prosperity visible on the surface masks the suffering of the farmers who are its foundation. Despite their hard work, farmers lack the economic security that has been promised for decades. Efforts to alleviate their debt burden have been insufficient. Although minimum support price (MSP) and other economic protections are claimed, intermediaries, traders, and powerful business lobbies prevent these benefits from reaching farmers. The widening gap between rich and poor starkly illustrates this grim reality.

Suicide is often seen as a last resort when all hope is lost, reflecting not only a person's despair with systemic disorder but also society's insensitivity. A person driven to suicide has clearly lost faith in society as well. These circumstances raise serious questions about the government's indifference and the failure of public welfare systems. In times of crisis, assistance systems are often ineffective. The desperation of small farmers, unable to meet their family responsibilities, drives them to such drastic actions. High inflation, unemployment, and diminishing job prospects in other sectors further exacerbate their misery.

The rising suicide rates call into question the effectiveness of government claims about providing free food grains to 800 million people. Why, in an era dubbed the "Amrit Kaal" of independence, are so many people driven to suicide? Serious efforts are needed to provide security for workers in the unorganized sector.

Establishing a Permanent Relief Mechanism for Farmers

It is ironic that, in a country celebrating its Azadi Ka Amrit Mahotsav, there is still no effective mechanism to compensate farmers for losses caused by seasonal disasters; everything operates on a temporary basis. After a disaster, political leaders distribute aid as if handing out alms. Farmers are also frustrated with the inadequate relief provided by insurance companies, leading some states to exclude their farmers from insurance schemes. In reality, these schemes have enriched insurance companies, while farmers continue to wait for genuine relief.

However, the Modi government's recent decision has provided some respite to farmers affected by last year's unseasonal rains. The Haryana government had informed the central government about the decline in crop quality due to rain and requested a relaxation of the procurement standards. In response, the central government decided to grant immediate relief, considering the complexity of the problem. The conditions for wheat procurement in Haryana were relaxed, allowing government agencies to procure wheat with up to 80% luster loss and 18% shriveled grains. Orders for procurement under these new rules have been issued to the relevant departmental officers, who have also been instructed to ensure smooth procurement in every market.

This year, wheat was sown over 22.9 lakh hectares in Haryana. Normally, the state produces an average of 45 to 50 quintals of wheat per hectare annually. However, unseasonal rains are expected to reduce this yield by 5 to 7 quintals per hectare. To mitigate the farmers' losses, the procurement rules were adjusted. Additionally, the state government has assured a special Girdawari during the assembly session to assess the crop damage and provide timely relief money.

Government assessments indicate that about 16 lakh acres of crops have been damaged by unseasonal rain and hailstorms. Consequently, despite the wheat procurement process starting on April 1, the mandis have not received much grain. To expedite the procurement process and boost farmers' morale, the state's deputy CM assured that the government would purchase every grain brought to the mandi. Compensation for damaged crops has also been outlined: Rs 15,000 per acre for over 75% damage, Rs 12,000 per acre for 51-75% damage, and Rs 9,000 per acre for 25-50% damage. The government also promised that payments would be made to farmers' accounts within 48 to 72 hours of crop purchase, with a 9% interest rate if payments are delayed.

However, given the daily damage to crops from natural calamities, there is a pressing need for a permanent and effective relief mechanism. Relief should be timely and based on clear, transparent criteria, rather than being a mere formality. Additionally, farmers must be educated about the significant weather changes due to climate change and motivated to adjust their crop cycles accordingly. Compensation and relief, while necessary, are not permanent solutions. A stable system must be established to determine fair compensation based on ground realities, ensuring that farmers are better prepared for future disasters.

Farmers Suffering from Misery

Despite numerous governmental claims of improving the conditions for farmers, the reality is that the agricultural sector's situation is deteriorating daily. Just a few years ago, the opposition frequently targeted governments over farmer suicides, leading to the development of various schemes such as crop insurance and easy-term agricultural loans. However, these schemes have provided little to no benefit. For many years, data on farmer suicides was not disclosed, creating the illusion that these tragic incidents had ceased. Unfortunately, the reality is quite different.

Last year, the Minister of State for Home Affairs revealed that in the past three years, seventeen thousand farmers had committed suicide, according to data from the National Crime Records Bureau (NCRB). The NCRB records details of accidental deaths and suicides reported by various police stations across the country, suggesting that these figures might be underestimated and the actual numbers could be higher.

The plight of farmers due to an incomplete market system in the country is well-known. As farming becomes increasingly unprofitable, many farmers are leaving villages in search of alternative livelihoods. The number of agricultural laborers is declining alarmingly across the nation. Despite the central government's claims of efforts to improve conditions for small and marginal farmers and double their incomes, the reality is that farmers are neither receiving fair prices for their crops nor satisfactory benefits from schemes like crop insurance. This ongoing struggle is why farmers have long demanded a law guaranteeing minimum support price (MSP).

After the year-long farmers' movement, the government promised to form a committee and introduce a law regarding MSP, but no steps have been taken in this direction, leading to renewed resentment among farmers. The escalating costs of fertilizers, seeds, irrigation, plowing, harvesting, and transportation are not matched by proportionate crop prices. Moreover, the government fails to ensure the purchase of the entire crop at these prices, leaving farmers at the mercy of middlemen.

The farmers' dire situation, compounded by an unjust market, ties directly to their increasing misery. Many farmers take loans to sow cash crops, but when crops fail due to weather vagaries, neither crop insurance schemes nor other means provide adequate compensation or help in repaying those loans. This increasing debt burden often leads farmers to take their own lives. Even a single farmer suicide due to agricultural losses should concern the government, but it seems to elicit little to no reaction from the authorities.

Income Will Increase with Market Improvement

To alleviate the suffering of farmers caused by market deficiencies, the Central Government announced an annual direct income support of Rs 6,000 to small farmers owning less than 2 hectares of land. Although this amount is minimal by any standard, this initiative represents a significant shift in recognizing agriculture's role in the country's economic progress. With this change, agricultural income policy has moved from being 'crop price-based' to 'income assurance.'

This step is expected to open new opportunities for farmers' progress in the agricultural sector.

In 2019, the Union Finance Minister allocated Rs 20,000 crore for this scheme, with an initial installment of Rs 2,000 reaching each beneficiary farmer's bank account. However, the farming community, facing numerous difficulties, has expressed dissatisfaction with this small amount of assistance.

It is questionable whether Rs 500 per month is sufficient to provide relief to the 12 crore families of small and marginal farmers facing a severe agrarian crisis. It is also unclear how this modest sum will address the issue of farmer suicides. News of farmer suicides surfaces almost daily. For instance, according to the Bharatiya Kisan Union, despite the initiation of loan waivers for 2 lakh farmers in Punjab since January 2018, 430 farmers committed suicide in the past year. This raises the question of whether this financial relief will indeed curb farmer suicides.

According to the All India Rural Finance Inclusive Survey (2016-17) conducted by NABARD, the average monthly income of a farmer in India is Rs 8,931. Thus, Rs 500 per month seems insufficient to stop farmer suicides. This direct income support of Rs 1,000 crore is neither adequate to double farmers' incomes nor enough for them to purchase essential farming supplies. The 2016 Economic Survey reveals that the average annual income of farmers in seventeen states is only Rs 20,000, translating to a monthly income of just Rs 1,700 for nearly half of the farming families in India. It is distressing to consider how millions of farmers survive on such a small amount.

The central government has modeled its direct income support on the Telangana government's scheme. Under the Pradhan Mantri Kisan Yojana, Rs 75,000 crore has been allocated, but there is no reason why this amount cannot be doubled. If so, the annual assistance per farmer family should increase from Rs 6,000 to Rs 12,000, doubling the central budget's burden to Rs 1.5 lakh crore. This raises the question of where this additional amount would come from. A viable solution would be to halt the annual subsidy of Rs 1.86 lakh crore given to industries, initially intended to support them after the 2008-09 global recession. This subsidy, no longer justified, has led to Rs 18.5 lakh crore being waived off. It is surprising that no questions are raised about this policy that has created a significant economic imbalance. Given the farmers' plight, why can't this money be redirected for their betterment?

Additionally, the central government's scheme benefits only land-owning farmers, unlike Telangana's 'Raitu Bandhu' scheme, which supports farmers proportional to their land, regardless of size. Excluding tenant farmers from this relief is ironic, as they constitute 40-50 percent of the total farming population. This large group is deprived of the benefits available to land-owning farmers.

It is encouraging that policymakers now acknowledge the need to provide direct income to farmers. However, farming remains under the control of a market system that has kept agricultural income stagnant for the past four decades.

Various surveys indicate that agricultural income has declined over time. Farming has been neglected in favor of economic reforms driven by multinational institutions. It is ironic that farmers bear the burden of keeping food prices low and providing cheap raw materials to industries.

An economic system that superficially supports agriculture while categorizing it as a non-economic activity needs to change. According to a credible study, the agriculture sector incurred a total loss of Rs 45 lakh crore between 2000 and 2017 due to elevated crop prices. If farmers had received fair prices for their produce during this period, Indian agriculture would be much more prosperous today. Government policymakers do not believe that agriculture alone can revive the country's economy and provide livelihoods for millions of families. However, addressing this could also alleviate pressure on the employment sector.

Providing direct income to small and marginal farmers is seen as the first step towards enhancing farming income. It is expected that this amount will be increased periodically. There have been calls for the establishment of a 'Farmers' Income Commission,' whose primary goal would be to ensure a respectable monthly income for farmers' families. This is believed to pave the way for greater public sector investment and further reforms in the agriculture sector, ultimately bringing prosperity to farmers' homes.

The Hidden Crisis in Agriculture

The dire state of agriculture has created a significant crisis, impacting related sectors and stalling overall progress. Recent studies indicate that income growth in non-agricultural sectors within rural areas has been minimal over the past five years. It's remarkable that rural India has managed to endure such a severe situation, even during the COVID-19 crisis, where any other sector would have collapsed or vanished entirely from the economic landscape.

Agriculture has faced numerous challenges over the past two decades, and the situation was similarly bleak even before that. According to a United Nations study, after accounting for inflation between 1985 and 2005, the prices farmers receive for their produce have remained virtually unchanged globally. For four decades, farming income has been stagnant. As a result, farmers are often born into debt and die in debt. In Indian agriculture, farm income has also stagnated. For instance, while the Minimum Support Price (MSP) for wheat rose from Rs. 76 per quintal in 1970 to Rs. 1450 per quintal in 2015, an increase of nineteen times, this pales in comparison to the income growth in government and other professions during the same period. Essentially, farmers are shouldering the burden of subsidies given to consumers. The financial strategies used to keep food grain prices low are ultimately at the farmers' expense.

Shocking Losses

Recently, it has become common to see farmers discarding tomatoes, potatoes, and onions on the streets due to not receiving fair prices. Headlines frequently report that farmers are not getting a fair market price for their produce, leading to a 20 to 40 percent drop in retail prices. According to the Shanta Kumar Committee report, only 6 percent of farmers in the country receive the minimum support price

(MSP). Announcing the MSP does not help set flour prices for consumers, nor does it guarantee that farmers will receive the declared price. The JCCP formula for setting the MSP aims not only to ensure farmers receive this price but also to prevent future inflation. However, microeconomic policies contribute significantly to the current agricultural crisis, often setting prices below the cost of production to keep food grain prices low.

The government's MSP calculation is based on an equation that includes the farmer's out-of-pocket costs at the time of sowing (A-2 cost) and wages paid to family and agricultural laborers (FL). This total cost is called A-2+FL. The government claims it sets the MSP by adding a 50 percent profit to these costs, in line with the Swaminathan Commission's recommendation to add a 50 percent profit to the total cost. However, the prices determined by this formula often do not reflect the actual target, and the government has not ensured that crops are not bought below the declared MSP. Farmer leaders have challenged the government's claims, and trade data shows that farmers frequently receive prices lower than the declared MSP in many markets, with evidence often appearing on social media.

The methodology for calculating the cost of crop production is rarely questioned, despite a comprehensive system tracking sowing, harvesting, and total production costs. The formula used for determining production costs differs significantly from that used for setting prices of commercial products, where every minor expense is included.

While workers in non-agricultural sectors receive 108 types of allowances in addition to dearness allowance, farmers do not benefit from similar considerations. Key allowances such as housing, transportation, health, and education are never included when setting commodity prices. Why is this the case? Farmers also need to provide for their families. These allowances could be incorporated into the MSP based on the total per-hectare cost or provided directly to farmers' accounts.

Social Impact

Depriving farmers of their rightful income has significant social repercussions, often tied to their escalating debt. According to the National Crime Records Bureau, 318,528 farmers committed suicide between 1995 and 2015, with debt being the primary cause of these continuous deaths. These factors collectively contribute to the disintegration of the social fabric.

Ironically, agricultural policy makers focus more on increasing crop production to ensure food grain availability remains adequate. However, increasing agricultural income has never received the necessary attention. Agriculture has been deliberately kept in a state of improvisation to sustain economic reforms.

Globally, policies are being designed to move people out of agriculture and create cheap labor for industries. These agricultural refugees end up crowding cities, forced to take on any work, no matter how menial, to survive. The stagnation of agricultural income over recent decades has led to a significant decrease in public sector investment in agriculture. Total investment from both public and private sectors in agriculture is steadily declining, while tax reliefs for the industrial sector continue to rise.

Government economic advisors consistently advocate for increased investment in industries to move youth out of agriculture. It is ironic that governments are neglecting agriculture, which is the backbone of life and livelihood for millions of villagers.

Convert joint accounts to sole ownership.

The issue of converting Mushtarka accounts to sole ownership is of significant importance to 70 to 80 percent of the country's farmers. Since independence, land ownership has been recorded in revenue documents in two ways: sole ownership and Mushtarka (joint) accounts. Some foresighted landowners, who had an understanding of the situation, divided their land and registered it under separate Khewat and Kila numbers as sole owners, ensuring peace of mind for their descendants. However, over time, families associated with Mushtarka accounts expanded, and the number of joint owners increased. As some of these owners sold their shares to outsiders, the Khewats became increasingly complicated, with more unknown individuals involved.

A further complication arose when some landowners took bank loans using Mushtarka accounts as collateral. Due to legal disputes, unregistered inheritance, and other errors, these accounts have become so complex that land division within these Khewats has become nearly impossible, even if desired. This situation has left many Indians living abroad, whose land is tied up in Mushtarka accounts, feeling helpless. In some cases, a single landowner's actions—such as failing to register a loan, litigation, or inheritance transfer—have affected all other joint owners and their heirs since 1947. This issue is expected to continue trapping future generations for the next 100 years.

Landowners of Mushtarka accounts live and die with the burden of worry, fear, and uncertainty. Although Khewats can technically be divided with the consent of all joint owners, the current problem is that some shareholders are unwilling to cooperate. This is a national problem, a complex one that urgently needs resolution. Converting Mushtarka accounts into sole ownership accounts is a critical step. No matter how many development projects the government undertakes for farmers, solving this issue would have a far greater impact than all other efforts combined.

First Listen to the Farmer, Then Understand the Problem

It's an irony in this agricultural country that while farmers are wooed for votes and their issues are highlighted to corner the central and state governments, there's little discussion on improving their economic condition. The critical question is whether we have the capacity to produce enough grains for our 140 crore population in the coming decades. Are our policies farsighted enough to avoid dependence on foreign countries for grains? The farmers' movement has stalled agricultural reform prospects. The opposition's strategy prioritizes political gains over the interests of farmers, agriculture, and the public. Constructive efforts by the government should be recognized in the country's interest.

Although the year-long farmers' movement halted the implementation of the three agricultural reform laws proposed by the Central Government, it also diminished the chances of future reformist laws for the next decade. While political parties may celebrate the government's defeat, the farmers have lost an opportunity for reforms. We need agricultural reforms to meet the 21st-century demands and address the food needs of 1.4 billion people while increasing farmers' income. The farmer movement near Delhi, mainly involving farmers from Punjab, Haryana, and Uttar Pradesh, was one of India's longest. The government's approach to the movement was not constructive. Even if the government's intentions were right, it failed to communicate the benefits of the reforms to the farmers. In the current economic turmoil, is it justified to tamper with the minimum support price (MSP)? Farmers should have been informed about the true intent of the reforms. Why do farmers feel the government is not adopting a liberal attitude in a democratic system? Why doesn't the government demonstrate sensitivity and magnanimity? Opposition leaders argue there was no need to introduce these bills secretly during the Corona crisis or pass them in a hurry.

The commercialization of agriculture has adversely affected small farmers globally. Can this model be effective in a country like India with small-holding farming? Global statistics show that commercialization has led farmers to lose their land. In India, agriculture is not just an industry; it's integral to a farmer's identity. For generations, land has been passed down within families. How can farmers compromise on its value? Farming is becoming increasingly unprofitable. Many farmers also rent land for cultivation, fearing that the new system will exclude them. The government should address these fears and listen to the farmers' real problems. Before implementing reforms, there should have been a nationwide debate, with the opinions of the farmers considered. Agriculture is a state subject, requiring extensive discussions with the states. Democracy does not allow for oligarchic traditions. Some farmer organizations suggest postponing reforms and introducing new draft laws after comprehensive discussions. While 21st-century agriculture cannot function like it did in the 16th century, the farmers' trust and opinions should be prioritized. Long-lasting movements are not in the best interest of society and the country.

Haryana and Punjab have been at the forefront of agricultural reforms. Punjab benefited significantly from post-independence development projects, such as the Bhakra and Nangal dams. The green revolution, facilitated by water availability, primarily benefited Punjab, Haryana, and Western Uttar Pradesh, which also reaped the benefits of the MSP. This is why the movement was more intense in these areas. Other regions, which did not benefit from the MSP, did not witness similar movements. The movement also had political and caste-related motivations, historically reacting against the government. Consequently, some farmers in Haryana and Punjab feel that the government is not sensitive to their plight.

Focus Should Be on Empowering Farmers

Once again, farmers in Punjab are protesting to demand legal status for the minimum support price (MSP). One solution is for the government to set the MSP and purchase all crops directly. Another option is for the government to ensure that grains are bought at the MSP in the open market. Post-Green Revolution, the government has been buying wheat, paddy, and some other crops at MSP in certain states. Some farmer leaders argue that the government wants to avoid buying at MSP, leaving farmers at the mercy of the market. The contention is that the government buys at MSP because it's either below or equal to the market price, suggesting that if buying all crops at MSP were economically viable, the government would have adopted this model seventy years ago. Alternatively, if the market were to buy crops at MSP, it would do so only as long as it remains profitable. The market will not buy at a higher support price, and no buyer can be compelled to purchase produce. If the market rejects the crops, who will bear the penalty?

Farmers have long demanded MSP legislation, but even if implemented, the open market cannot be restricted to a fixed price. The market will ultimately determine crop prices. Incomplete markets like India cannot fully realize the concept of MSP. Another option is for the government to set and buy all crops at MSP, but if this were feasible, it would have been adopted globally. The government's hesitation to implement MSP laws indicates it's not feasible or in the national interest. A decade has passed in this dilemma, and it may persist. The government should clearly communicate to farmers that this is not implementable.

If farmers believe the government will buy all crops at the minimum price, then steps should be taken; otherwise, agricultural products should be sold based on market dynamics. Efforts to improve the market must be prioritized. Farmers need to understand that their earnings depend on the market and should not rely heavily on government support. The government has limited capacity to offer substantial aid. Farmers should align their methods and livelihoods with the market. My suggestion is to take some experimental steps for two years. First, the government should enact an MSP law and test if it can compel the market to buy crops at MSP. Secondly, the government should purchase as many crops as possible at MSP and assess its capacity to buy all crops.

Farmers face multiple challenges. Land division across generations results in smaller holdings, making profitable farming difficult. Hence, MSP is seen as a lifeline. For instance, in the 1980s, a classmate's father and his brother owned 30 acres of fertile land, a prosperous family. Over time, land was sold to meet household expenses, and divisions reduced profitability. A national campaign, "One Farmer, One Heir," could be beneficial.

Another issue is the impact of the new consumerist culture on farmers, where they are encouraged to take loans recklessly. Until 2000, farmers received small loans from government banks for household needs. Many borrowed from moneylenders. Those with sufficient income repaid loans; others struggled and sold land. Around 2000, farmers would take out large loans for expensive tractors, only to sell them at a loss and repay the bank later.

Empowering Farmers: A Practical Approach

Back in the day, I advised farmers to sell a small portion of their land (from one kanal to one acre) to meet immediate needs instead of incurring heavy losses of one to two lakhs. This way, they could preserve the majority of their land. Some farmers followed this advice, while others did not, resulting in the sale of large parts of their land later. Even now, farmers have the same approach to loans, believing they can take a loan and repay it later. Today, farmers are demanding loan waivers from the government. Even if the government agrees to this, the cycle of taking loans will restart on the same path. My suggestion is to raise awareness at the national level about taking loans sensibly. Farmers should borrow only what they can easily repay. Without resources to repay excessive loans, only their lands will be sold. Ultimately, the decision lies with the farmers.

Currently, the government maintains MSP to control inflation and support small farmers, mainly for Kharif and Rabi crops. The question arises whether other crops should also fall under MSP. However, it is a harsh reality that without democratic pressure, governments might discontinue MSP. This concern was heightened during recent farmers' movements, leading to persistent demands for MSP to be legally enforced. Small farmers, who depend on small holdings, cannot be left to market fluctuations. Even though only six percent of farmers benefit from MSP, its absence could worsen market conditions. While governments seek alternatives to MSP, the existence of small farmers could be threatened if MSP is abolished.

Thus, the question remains why major schemes to increase farmers' income have not materialized. There should be discussions on the reality of promises like doubling farmers' income by 2022. Real income should be assessed considering inflation. According to the National Sample Survey Office, the estimated monthly income of a farmer family in 2018-19 was only Rs 10,218, while the cost of agricultural inputs like fertilizers, pesticides, and diesel has nearly doubled in recent years.

The current MSP scheme needs to be enhanced and made more effective. More farmers should benefit from MSP on all twenty-three crops under the system. Farmers demand a legal guarantee for MSP due to a lack of government accountability towards it.

The challenges facing agriculture in the country are well understood. Increasing farmers' income will help eradicate poverty. The agricultural crisis should be approached humanely to improve the quality of life for farmers and farm laborers. Policymakers must remember that farming is not just a business or economic trade in Indian society. When Gandhi said the soul of the country resides in villages, it had profound meaning. For a significant population in India, farming is a way of life passed down for generations. It's tied to their heritage and the future of their descendants.

Seeds of Prosperity and Misery for Farmers

The financial condition of farmers in the country can generally be divided into two broad categories:

The first category consists of farmers who have fertile land, sufficient irrigation facilities, stable crop productivity, and a steady market demand for their crops. The prices for their crops remain stable, and the government provides the facility of Minimum Support Price (MSP). Regardless of whether these farmers have small or large land holdings, their income remains stable. Additionally, smallholding farmers in this category often diversify by growing flowers and vegetables alongside their main crops. Farmers who have established additional sources of income beyond farming also enjoy a certain level of financial security.

The second category includes farmers who lack fertile land and adequate water resources. These farmers face significant fluctuations in crop productivity and prices. Regardless of their land holdings, their financial condition remains poor throughout the country. Efforts should be focused on addressing the problems and crises faced by farmers in this category.

Community Support in Times of Crisis

It is often observed that farmers, unable to get a fair price and find buyers, end up discarding fruits and vegetables on the roads. During such times, the public should step in to help. Rather than offering mere verbal sympathy, tangible steps should be taken to assist them. For instance, citizens could collectively purchase one or two kilos of vegetables and fruits each, helping farmers mitigate their losses.

Implementing Recommendations

Bharat Ratna agricultural scientist M.S. Swaminathan proposed a good formula for ensuring fair crop prices for farmers, but even he did not provide a clear solution for implementing it on the ground. While the government offers various concessions, subsidies, and loan waivers to support farmers, and farmers' organizations run campaigns advocating for farmers' rights, these efforts alone are insufficient. Farmers, like traders, laborers, and professionals, must seek their income from the market. Therefore, they should not rely solely on government support and policies. Alternative measures involving the private sector should be explored. Although these reforms should have been implemented three decades ago, it is crucial to start now.

Government's Role in Finding Solutions

Farmers are demanding legal status for MSP. However, in an incomplete market, we cannot control market dynamics entirely; the market ultimately determines the price of food grains. One viable option is for the government to purchase all crops at a fixed price. Ultimately, the issues of loan waivers and legal status for MSP, along with government purchasing of crops, need to be resolved through dialogue between the government and farmers.

The Country Should Also Bear the Cost of Straw Disposal

The issue of paddy straw disposal has been a persistent problem for many years. The government aims to eliminate pollution and preserve soil fertility by discouraging the burning of straw. However, this conflict remains unresolved. The government expects farmers to bear the cost of straw disposal, but farmers are unwilling to shoulder this expense. Although the government provides various financial incentives for straw disposal, farmers still incur significant costs. This year, farmers spent around three thousand rupees on cutting the straw, with twenty-three hundred rupees for machine cutting and seven hundred rupees for bundling. With an average paddy yield of approximately twenty-two quintals per fort, the disposal cost per quintal ranges from one hundred to one hundred twenty-five rupees. The government should include this expense in the MSP and compensate farmers accordingly. Farmers should be informed that this cost is covered, and they should avoid burning stubble. The burden of this cost should be shared by consumers nationwide, not just the farmers.

Farmers Keeping Pace with the Times

It is important to recognize that farmers have strived to contribute their best to the country despite limited resources, technology, knowledge, and economic conditions. Today's young farmers are educated, aware of global agricultural practices and markets, and willing to adopt new technologies. The government and society must provide them with better facilities and opportunities to help them stay current with evolving times.

Making Small Holdings Profitable

Over time, the majority of farmers' land holdings have become very small, making it difficult to cover household expenses after accounting for costs. The impracticality of small-holding farming may be contributing to the increase in farmer suicides. The government needs to act swiftly to make small-holding farming profitable.

Unified Effort for Farmers' Welfare

Recently, there was a significant conflict between the government and farmer organizations over agricultural reforms. It is essential for both parties to come together on a common platform for the welfare of farmers, setting aside past disagreements and avoiding further delays.

Issue a White Paper on Reforms

The world is currently experiencing a population crisis, and India, in particular, has seen rapid population growth.

Despite the increased demand for food products, farmers are not receiving fair prices for their crops. The government needs to seriously examine why this is happening and identify any flaws in the current system.

I believe it is essential for the government to communicate its perspectives to the farmers. Additionally, both farmer organizations and the government should present a comprehensive white paper to the nation. This document should outline the necessary steps and new laws required to improve the conditions for farmers and address all matters related to their interests.

Milton Keynes UK
Ingram Content Group UK Ltd.
UKHW050644051124
450710UK00026B/243